50 Family Dinner Time Recipes

By: Kelly Johnson

Table of Contents

- Spaghetti Bolognese
- Chicken Alfredo
- Beef Tacos
- Lasagna
- Stir-fried Chicken and Vegetables
- Meatloaf with Mashed Potatoes
- Chicken Parmesan
- BBQ Ribs with Corn on the Cob
- Sloppy Joes
- Beef Stew
- Chicken Pot Pie
- Grilled Salmon with Asparagus
- Shrimp Scampi
- Chicken and Rice Casserole
- Pork Chops with Apple Sauce
- Beef and Broccoli Stir-fry
- Chili Con Carne
- Chicken Fajitas
- Fish Tacos
- Beef Enchiladas
- Homemade Pizza
- Macaroni and Cheese
- Shepherd's Pie
- Teriyaki Chicken
- Stuffed Bell Peppers
- Meatball Sub Sandwiches
- Chicken Caesar Salad
- Grilled Chicken with Roasted Vegetables
- Eggplant Parmesan
- Beef and Vegetable Stir-fry
- Sweet and Sour Chicken
- Chicken and Dumplings
- Shrimp Fried Rice
- Chicken Quesadillas
- Lemon Garlic Roasted Chicken
- Baked Ziti
- Fish and Chips
- Beef Burritos
- Turkey Meatballs with Spaghetti
- Chicken Tenders with Honey Mustard
- Broccoli and Cheddar Stuffed Chicken
- Beef Stroganoff

- Grilled Steak with Roasted Potatoes
- Chicken and Vegetable Soup
- Baked Chicken Wings
- Beef and Cheese Tacos
- Spaghetti Carbonara
- Baked Salmon with Lemon and Dill
- Pork Tenderloin with Roasted Brussels Sprouts
- Vegetarian Stir-fry

Spaghetti Bolognese

Ingredients:

- 1 lb ground beef or pork
- 1 onion, finely chopped
- 2 cloves garlic, minced
- 1 carrot, finely grated or chopped
- 1 celery stalk, finely chopped
- 1 can (14 oz) crushed tomatoes
- 1/4 cup red wine (optional)
- 1/4 cup milk or cream (optional for richness)
- 1 tsp dried oregano
- 1 tsp dried basil
- Salt and pepper to taste
- 1 tbsp olive oil
- Fresh parsley or basil, chopped (for garnish)
- 1 lb spaghetti

Instructions:

1. Heat olive oil in a large pan over medium heat. Add chopped onion, carrot, and celery, and sauté for about 5 minutes until softened.
2. Add garlic and cook for an additional minute.
3. Stir in the ground beef or pork, breaking it up with a spoon as it browns. Cook for 6-8 minutes until the meat is browned and no longer pink.
4. Add red wine (if using), scraping up any bits from the bottom of the pan, and let it reduce for 2-3 minutes.
5. Pour in crushed tomatoes, oregano, basil, and a pinch of salt and pepper. Stir to combine, then let the sauce simmer on low heat for 30-45 minutes to develop flavors.

6. Near the end of the cooking time, bring a large pot of salted water to a boil. Add spaghetti and cook according to package instructions. Drain and set aside.

7. Stir in milk or cream if you want a richer sauce, adjust seasoning with salt and pepper to taste.

8. Serve the sauce over the spaghetti, garnished with fresh parsley or basil.

Chicken Alfredo

Ingredients:

- 2 boneless, skinless chicken breasts
- 1 tbsp olive oil
- 2 cloves garlic, minced
- 1 cup heavy cream
- 1/2 cup grated Parmesan cheese
- 1/4 cup grated mozzarella cheese
- Salt and pepper to taste
- 1 tbsp butter
- 1 lb fettuccine pasta
- Fresh parsley, chopped (for garnish)

Instructions:

1. Cook fettuccine according to package instructions. Drain and set aside.
2. Heat olive oil in a pan over medium heat. Season chicken breasts with salt and pepper, then cook for 6-7 minutes per side until golden and cooked through. Slice into strips.
3. In the same pan, melt butter over medium heat. Add garlic and cook for 1 minute.
4. Pour in the heavy cream, bringing it to a simmer. Add Parmesan and mozzarella cheese, stirring until smooth. Season with salt and pepper.
5. Add the cooked pasta and sliced chicken, stirring to coat. Garnish with fresh parsley and serve.

Beef Tacos

Ingredients:

- 1 lb ground beef
- 1 small onion, finely chopped
- 1 packet taco seasoning
- 1/4 cup water
- 8 taco shells or tortillas
- Lettuce, shredded
- Tomatoes, diced
- Shredded cheddar cheese
- Salsa and sour cream (optional)

Instructions:

1. In a pan, cook ground beef and onion over medium heat until browned. Drain excess fat.
2. Stir in taco seasoning and water. Simmer for 5 minutes until the sauce thickens.
3. Warm taco shells according to package instructions. Fill with seasoned beef and top with lettuce, tomatoes, cheese, and any other desired toppings.

Lasagna

Ingredients:

- 1 lb ground beef or pork
- 1 onion, chopped
- 2 cloves garlic, minced
- 1 can (15 oz) tomato sauce
- 1 can (6 oz) tomato paste
- 1 can (14 oz) diced tomatoes
- 1 tsp dried oregano
- 1 tsp dried basil
- 1/2 tsp salt
- 1/2 tsp black pepper
- 12 lasagna noodles, cooked
- 2 cups ricotta cheese
- 2 cups shredded mozzarella cheese
- 1/2 cup grated Parmesan cheese
- 1 egg, beaten

Instructions:

1. Preheat oven to 375°F (190°C).
2. Brown the ground beef with onion and garlic. Stir in tomato sauce, paste, diced tomatoes, oregano, basil, salt, and pepper. Simmer for 20 minutes.
3. In a bowl, mix ricotta cheese, mozzarella, Parmesan, and the beaten egg.
4. Spread a thin layer of sauce in the bottom of a baking dish. Layer with noodles, cheese mixture, and sauce. Repeat layers until all ingredients are used.
5. Cover with foil and bake for 25 minutes. Remove foil and bake for an additional 15 minutes until bubbly and golden.

Stir-fried Chicken and Vegetables

Ingredients:

- 2 boneless, skinless chicken breasts, sliced into strips
- 1 tbsp soy sauce
- 1 tbsp oyster sauce
- 1 tbsp sesame oil
- 1 bell pepper, sliced
- 1 carrot, sliced thin
- 1 zucchini, sliced
- 1/2 onion, sliced
- 2 cloves garlic, minced
- Cooked rice (for serving)

Instructions:

1. Heat sesame oil in a large pan over medium-high heat. Add chicken and cook until browned and cooked through. Remove and set aside.
2. In the same pan, add garlic, onion, bell pepper, carrot, and zucchini. Stir-fry for 5-7 minutes until vegetables are tender.
3. Return chicken to the pan. Stir in soy sauce and oyster sauce, cooking for another 2 minutes.
4. Serve stir-fried chicken and vegetables over cooked rice.

Meatloaf with Mashed Potatoes

Ingredients:

- 1 lb ground beef
- 1 egg
- 1/2 cup breadcrumbs
- 1/4 cup milk
- 1 small onion, chopped
- 1 tbsp Worcestershire sauce
- 1/4 cup ketchup
- Salt and pepper to taste
- 4 large potatoes, peeled and cubed
- 2 tbsp butter
- 1/2 cup milk (for mashed potatoes)
- Salt and pepper to taste

Instructions:

1. Preheat oven to 375°F (190°C). In a bowl, mix ground beef, egg, breadcrumbs, milk, onion, Worcestershire sauce, ketchup, salt, and pepper. Shape into a loaf and place in a baking dish.
2. Bake for 50-60 minutes, until cooked through.
3. While meatloaf bakes, cook potatoes in salted water until tender, about 15 minutes. Drain, then mash with butter, milk, salt, and pepper. Serve with meatloaf.

Chicken Parmesan

Ingredients:

- 4 boneless, skinless chicken breasts
- 1 cup breadcrumbs
- 1/2 cup grated Parmesan cheese
- 1 egg, beaten
- 1 cup marinara sauce
- 1 1/2 cups shredded mozzarella cheese
- Olive oil for frying
- Fresh basil for garnish

Instructions:

1. Preheat oven to 375°F (190°C). Mix breadcrumbs and Parmesan cheese. Dip chicken breasts in beaten egg, then coat with breadcrumb mixture.
2. Heat olive oil in a pan and fry chicken until golden brown on both sides. Remove and place on a baking sheet.
3. Top each chicken breast with marinara sauce and mozzarella cheese. Bake for 20 minutes or until cheese is melted and bubbly.
4. Garnish with fresh basil and serve.

BBQ Ribs with Corn on the Cob

Ingredients:

- 2 racks of baby back ribs
- 1/4 cup BBQ rub (store-bought or homemade)
- 1 cup BBQ sauce
- 4 ears of corn, husked
- 1 tbsp butter (for corn)
- Salt and pepper to taste

Instructions:

1. Preheat oven to 300°F (150°C). Rub ribs with BBQ rub, then wrap in foil. Bake for 2.5-3 hours.
2. While ribs bake, bring a pot of water to a boil and cook corn for 10-12 minutes until tender. Drain and brush with butter.
3. After ribs finish baking, remove foil, brush with BBQ sauce, and broil for 5 minutes.
4. Serve ribs with corn on the cob.

Sloppy Joes

Ingredients:

- 1 lb ground beef
- 1 onion, chopped
- 1/2 cup ketchup
- 1/4 cup Worcestershire sauce
- 1 tbsp mustard
- 1 tbsp brown sugar
- Salt and pepper to taste
- 4 hamburger buns

Instructions:

1. Brown ground beef and onion in a pan over medium heat. Drain excess fat.
2. Stir in ketchup, Worcestershire sauce, mustard, brown sugar, salt, and pepper. Simmer for 10 minutes until thickened.
3. Serve on hamburger buns.

Beef Stew

Ingredients:

- 1 lb beef stew meat, cubed
- 2 tbsp flour
- 4 cups beef broth
- 1 onion, chopped
- 3 carrots, sliced
- 3 potatoes, cubed
- 2 cloves garlic, minced
- 2 tsp dried thyme
- Salt and pepper to taste

Instructions:

1. Toss beef cubes in flour and brown in a pot over medium heat.
2. Add broth, onion, carrots, potatoes, garlic, thyme, salt, and pepper. Bring to a simmer.
3. Cover and cook for 1.5-2 hours until beef is tender. Serve warm.

Chicken Pot Pie

Ingredients:

- 2 cups cooked, diced chicken
- 1 cup frozen peas and carrots
- 1/4 cup butter
- 1/4 cup flour
- 2 cups chicken broth
- 1/2 cup milk
- 1 tsp dried thyme
- Salt and pepper to taste
- 1 package refrigerated pie crusts

Instructions:

1. Preheat oven to 400°F (200°C). In a pan, melt butter and whisk in flour. Cook for 2 minutes, then slowly add broth and milk.
2. Stir in chicken, peas, carrots, thyme, salt, and pepper. Simmer until thickened, about 5 minutes.
3. Roll out pie crusts and line a pie dish. Pour filling into crust, top with second crust, and crimp edges. Cut slits in the top crust.
4. Bake for 30-35 minutes until golden brown. Let cool before serving.

Grilled Salmon with Asparagus

Ingredients:

- 4 salmon fillets
- 1 bunch asparagus, trimmed
- 2 tbsp olive oil
- 1 lemon, sliced
- Salt and pepper to taste

Instructions:

1. Preheat grill to medium-high heat. Brush salmon and asparagus with olive oil, then season with salt and pepper.
2. Grill salmon for 4-5 minutes per side. Grill asparagus for 2-3 minutes, turning occasionally.
3. Serve salmon with grilled asparagus and lemon slices.

Shrimp Scampi

Ingredients:

- 1 lb shrimp, peeled and deveined
- 4 cloves garlic, minced
- 1/4 cup white wine
- 1/4 cup lemon juice
- 1/2 cup butter
- 2 tbsp olive oil
- 1 tbsp chopped parsley
- 1 lb spaghetti

Instructions:

1. Cook spaghetti according to package instructions. Drain and set aside.
2. In a pan, heat olive oil and butter. Add garlic and shrimp, cooking until shrimp turn pink.
3. Add white wine and lemon juice, simmer for 2 minutes. Toss shrimp with cooked spaghetti and garnish with parsley.

Chicken and Rice Casserole

Ingredients:

- 2 cups cooked chicken, shredded
- 1 cup rice
- 2 cups chicken broth
- 1 cup cream of mushroom soup
- 1/2 cup shredded cheddar cheese
- 1/2 cup frozen peas

Instructions:

1. Preheat oven to 350°F (175°C). In a bowl, combine chicken, rice, chicken broth, soup, and peas. Season with salt and pepper.
2. Transfer mixture to a greased casserole dish, top with cheddar cheese.
3. Bake for 25-30 minutes until bubbly and cheese is melted.

Pork Chops with Apple Sauce

Ingredients:

- 4 bone-in pork chops
- 1 tbsp olive oil
- 1 tsp dried thyme
- 2 apples, sliced
- 1/2 cup apple cider
- 1 tbsp brown sugar
- Salt and pepper to taste

Instructions:

1. Heat olive oil in a pan over medium-high heat. Season pork chops with thyme, salt, and pepper, and cook for 4-5 minutes per side until browned.

2. Remove pork chops and add apple slices, apple cider, and brown sugar to the pan. Simmer for 5 minutes until apples are tender.

3. Return pork chops to the pan, cooking for an additional 5 minutes to heat through. Serve with apple sauce.

Beef and Broccoli Stir-fry

Ingredients:

- 1 lb flank steak, sliced thinly
- 1 tbsp soy sauce
- 1 tbsp oyster sauce
- 1 tbsp cornstarch
- 2 tbsp vegetable oil
- 3 cups broccoli florets
- 2 cloves garlic, minced
- 1 tbsp ginger, grated
- 2 tbsp soy sauce
- 1 tbsp sesame oil
- 1/4 cup beef broth
- Salt and pepper to taste

Instructions:

1. In a bowl, mix beef, soy sauce, oyster sauce, and cornstarch. Let marinate for 10 minutes.
2. Heat vegetable oil in a pan over medium-high heat. Add broccoli and stir-fry for 3-4 minutes until tender. Remove and set aside.
3. In the same pan, add garlic and ginger, cooking for 1 minute. Add beef and stir-fry until browned.
4. Pour in soy sauce, sesame oil, and beef broth. Cook for another 2-3 minutes, then return broccoli to the pan and toss to combine. Serve hot.

Chili Con Carne

Ingredients:

- 1 lb ground beef
- 1 onion, chopped
- 2 cloves garlic, minced
- 1 can (15 oz) kidney beans, drained
- 1 can (15 oz) black beans, drained
- 1 can (14 oz) diced tomatoes
- 1 tbsp chili powder
- 1 tsp cumin
- 1/2 tsp paprika
- Salt and pepper to taste
- 1 tbsp olive oil
- Shredded cheddar cheese and sour cream for topping

Instructions:

1. Heat olive oil in a pot over medium heat. Brown ground beef with onion and garlic.
2. Stir in chili powder, cumin, paprika, salt, and pepper. Cook for 1-2 minutes until fragrant.
3. Add beans, tomatoes, and a cup of water. Simmer for 30 minutes, stirring occasionally.
4. Serve with shredded cheddar cheese and sour cream.

Chicken Fajitas

Ingredients:

- 2 boneless, skinless chicken breasts, sliced into strips
- 1 bell pepper, sliced
- 1 onion, sliced
- 2 tbsp olive oil
- 1 tsp chili powder
- 1 tsp cumin
- 1 tsp garlic powder
- Salt and pepper to taste
- 4 flour tortillas
- Sour cream and salsa for topping

Instructions:

1. Heat olive oil in a pan over medium heat. Add chicken and cook for 5-7 minutes until browned. Remove and set aside.
2. In the same pan, add bell pepper and onion. Stir-fry until tender, about 3-4 minutes.
3. Add the chicken back to the pan, then stir in chili powder, cumin, garlic powder, salt, and pepper.
4. Warm tortillas and fill with chicken and vegetable mixture. Top with sour cream and salsa.

Fish Tacos

Ingredients:

- 1 lb white fish fillets (such as tilapia or cod)
- 1 tbsp olive oil
- 1 tsp chili powder
- 1/2 tsp cumin
- Salt and pepper to taste
- 8 small corn tortillas
- 1 cup shredded cabbage
- 1/2 cup sour cream
- 1 tbsp lime juice
- Fresh cilantro for garnish

Instructions:

1. Preheat oven to 375°F (190°C). Brush fish fillets with olive oil and season with chili powder, cumin, salt, and pepper.
2. Bake fish for 10-12 minutes until flaky.
3. Warm tortillas in a dry skillet. Flake the fish and place on tortillas.
4. Mix sour cream and lime juice, then drizzle over the fish. Top with shredded cabbage and fresh cilantro.

Beef Enchiladas

Ingredients:

- 1 lb ground beef
- 1 onion, chopped
- 2 cups red enchilada sauce
- 8 corn tortillas
- 2 cups shredded cheddar cheese
- 1 tbsp olive oil
- 1 tsp cumin
- Salt and pepper to taste
- Fresh cilantro for garnish

Instructions:

1. Preheat oven to 350°F (175°C). Brown ground beef with onion in olive oil. Stir in cumin, salt, and pepper.
2. Warm tortillas in a dry skillet. Roll up a little beef mixture and cheese in each tortilla and place in a baking dish.
3. Pour enchilada sauce over the rolled tortillas and top with remaining cheese.
4. Bake for 20 minutes until cheese is melted and bubbly. Garnish with fresh cilantro.

Homemade Pizza

Ingredients:

- 1 pizza dough (store-bought or homemade)
- 1 cup pizza sauce
- 2 cups shredded mozzarella cheese
- Toppings of your choice (pepperoni, mushrooms, bell peppers, olives, etc.)
- Olive oil for brushing

Instructions:

1. Preheat oven to 475°F (245°C). Roll out pizza dough on a floured surface.
2. Spread pizza sauce on the dough, leaving a small border around the edges.
3. Sprinkle cheese evenly over the sauce and add your favorite toppings.
4. Bake for 10-12 minutes until the crust is golden and the cheese is bubbly.
5. Brush the crust with olive oil and serve.

Macaroni and Cheese

Ingredients:

- 8 oz elbow macaroni
- 2 tbsp butter
- 2 tbsp flour
- 2 cups milk
- 2 cups shredded cheddar cheese
- Salt and pepper to taste
- 1/2 tsp paprika (optional)

Instructions:

1. Cook macaroni according to package instructions. Drain and set aside.
2. In a saucepan, melt butter and whisk in flour. Cook for 1-2 minutes, then slowly add milk, whisking constantly until thickened.
3. Stir in cheese until melted and smooth. Season with salt, pepper, and paprika.
4. Toss the cooked macaroni in the cheese sauce and serve.

Shepherd's Pie

Ingredients:

- 1 lb ground beef or lamb
- 1 onion, chopped
- 2 carrots, diced
- 1 cup peas
- 1/4 cup beef broth
- 2 tbsp tomato paste
- 4 large potatoes, peeled and cubed
- 1/4 cup butter
- 1/2 cup milk
- Salt and pepper to taste

Instructions:

1. Preheat oven to 375°F (190°C). Brown ground beef or lamb with onion and carrots. Stir in peas, beef broth, and tomato paste. Simmer for 10 minutes.
2. Boil potatoes in salted water until tender, then mash with butter, milk, salt, and pepper.
3. Spread the meat mixture in a baking dish and top with mashed potatoes. Bake for 20 minutes until golden brown.

Teriyaki Chicken

Ingredients:

- 4 boneless, skinless chicken breasts
- 1/4 cup soy sauce
- 1/4 cup honey
- 2 tbsp rice vinegar
- 2 cloves garlic, minced
- 1 tbsp grated ginger
- 1 tbsp sesame oil
- 1 tbsp cornstarch (optional, for thickening)

Instructions:

1. In a bowl, whisk together soy sauce, honey, rice vinegar, garlic, ginger, and sesame oil. Marinate chicken in the mixture for 30 minutes.
2. Heat a skillet over medium heat and cook chicken for 6-7 minutes per side until cooked through.
3. If you prefer a thicker sauce, remove the chicken, whisk cornstarch into the sauce, and simmer for 2 minutes.
4. Serve the chicken with the sauce drizzled over and garnish with sesame seeds or green onions.

Stuffed Bell Peppers

Ingredients:

- 4 large bell peppers, tops cut off and seeds removed
- 1 lb ground beef or turkey
- 1 cup cooked rice
- 1 small onion, chopped
- 1 can (14 oz) diced tomatoes
- 1/2 cup shredded cheese (cheddar or mozzarella)
- 1 tbsp Italian seasoning
- Salt and pepper to taste
- 1 tbsp olive oil

Instructions:

1. Preheat oven to 375°F (190°C). Heat olive oil in a pan over medium heat. Cook ground meat with onion until browned.
2. Stir in cooked rice, diced tomatoes, Italian seasoning, salt, and pepper. Cook for another 5 minutes.
3. Stuff the peppers with the meat and rice mixture. Place in a baking dish and top with cheese.
4. Cover with foil and bake for 30 minutes. Remove foil and bake for an additional 10 minutes to melt the cheese.

Meatball Sub Sandwiches

Ingredients:

- 1 lb ground beef or turkey
- 1/2 cup breadcrumbs
- 1/4 cup Parmesan cheese
- 1 egg
- 1 tsp garlic powder
- 1 tsp dried oregano
- 1/2 tsp salt
- 1 jar marinara sauce
- 4 sub rolls
- 1 1/2 cups shredded mozzarella cheese

Instructions:

1. Preheat oven to 375°F (190°C). In a bowl, combine ground meat, breadcrumbs, Parmesan, egg, garlic powder, oregano, and salt. Form into meatballs.
2. Place meatballs on a baking sheet and bake for 20-25 minutes, until cooked through.
3. While meatballs bake, heat marinara sauce in a pan. Once meatballs are done, add them to the sauce and simmer for 5 minutes.
4. Split sub rolls and place meatballs inside. Top with mozzarella cheese and bake for 5-7 minutes until the cheese is melted.

Chicken Caesar Salad

Ingredients:

- 2 boneless, skinless chicken breasts
- 4 cups romaine lettuce, chopped
- 1/4 cup Caesar dressing
- 1/4 cup grated Parmesan cheese
- 1 cup croutons
- Salt and pepper to taste
- Olive oil for cooking

Instructions:

1. Season chicken breasts with salt and pepper. Heat olive oil in a pan over medium heat and cook chicken for 6-7 minutes per side, until golden and cooked through.
2. Let chicken rest for a few minutes, then slice into strips.
3. Toss lettuce with Caesar dressing, Parmesan cheese, and croutons. Top with sliced chicken and serve.

Grilled Chicken with Roasted Vegetables

Ingredients:

- 4 boneless, skinless chicken breasts
- 2 cups mixed vegetables (carrots, bell peppers, zucchini, etc.), chopped
- 2 tbsp olive oil
- 1 tsp garlic powder
- 1 tsp dried thyme
- Salt and pepper to taste

Instructions:

1. Preheat grill to medium-high heat. Season chicken with garlic powder, thyme, salt, and pepper.
2. Toss chopped vegetables with olive oil, salt, and pepper. Spread them on a baking sheet and roast at 400°F (200°C) for 20-25 minutes.
3. Grill chicken for 6-7 minutes per side, until cooked through.
4. Serve chicken with roasted vegetables.

Eggplant Parmesan

Ingredients:

- 2 large eggplants, sliced into 1/2-inch rounds
- 1 cup breadcrumbs
- 1/2 cup grated Parmesan cheese
- 2 cups marinara sauce
- 1 1/2 cups shredded mozzarella cheese
- 1 egg, beaten
- Olive oil for frying

Instructions:

1. Preheat oven to 375°F (190°C). Dip eggplant slices in beaten egg, then coat with breadcrumbs and Parmesan cheese.
2. Heat olive oil in a pan over medium heat. Fry eggplant slices until golden brown on both sides. Remove and set aside.
3. In a baking dish, layer eggplant slices, marinara sauce, and mozzarella cheese. Repeat layers.
4. Bake for 20-25 minutes, until cheese is melted and bubbly. Serve hot.

Beef and Vegetable Stir-fry

Ingredients:

- 1 lb beef sirloin or flank steak, sliced thinly
- 2 tbsp soy sauce
- 1 tbsp hoisin sauce
- 1 tbsp oyster sauce
- 2 tbsp vegetable oil
- 1 onion, sliced
- 2 bell peppers, sliced
- 1 cup snap peas
- 2 cloves garlic, minced
- 1 tsp ginger, grated
- Salt and pepper to taste

Instructions:

1. In a bowl, combine beef with soy sauce, hoisin sauce, and oyster sauce. Let marinate for 10 minutes.
2. Heat vegetable oil in a pan over medium-high heat. Stir-fry beef for 2-3 minutes until browned. Remove and set aside.
3. Add onion, bell peppers, snap peas, garlic, and ginger to the pan and stir-fry for 3-4 minutes until tender.
4. Return beef to the pan, toss to combine, and cook for an additional 2 minutes. Serve with rice.

Sweet and Sour Chicken

Ingredients:

- 2 boneless, skinless chicken breasts, cut into bite-sized pieces
- 1 cup flour
- 2 eggs, beaten
- 1/4 cup vegetable oil
- 1/2 cup pineapple chunks
- 1/4 cup bell pepper, chopped
- 1/4 cup onion, chopped
- 1/4 cup rice vinegar
- 1/4 cup ketchup
- 1/4 cup soy sauce
- 1/4 cup sugar

Instructions:

1. Preheat oven to 375°F (190°C). Coat chicken pieces in flour, then dip in egg and fry in vegetable oil for 4-5 minutes until golden brown. Remove and set aside.
2. In a bowl, mix rice vinegar, ketchup, soy sauce, and sugar. Stir until sugar dissolves.
3. Heat sauce in a pan, then add pineapple, bell pepper, and onion. Cook for 2-3 minutes.
4. Add fried chicken to the pan and toss to coat in the sauce. Serve with rice.

Chicken and Dumplings

Ingredients:

- 2 boneless, skinless chicken breasts, cooked and shredded
- 4 cups chicken broth
- 1 cup milk
- 2 carrots, diced
- 2 celery stalks, diced
- 1 small onion, chopped
- 2 cups all-purpose flour
- 1 tbsp baking powder
- 1/2 tsp salt
- 1/2 cup milk (for dumplings)
- 1/4 cup butter
- 1/4 cup chopped parsley

Instructions:

1. In a pot, bring chicken broth and milk to a boil. Add carrots, celery, and onion. Simmer for 15 minutes until vegetables are tender.
2. In a bowl, mix flour, baking powder, salt, milk, and butter to make dumpling dough.
3. Drop spoonfuls of dough into the simmering broth. Cover and cook for 10-12 minutes, until dumplings are cooked through.
4. Add shredded chicken and parsley. Stir to combine and serve.

Shrimp Fried Rice

Ingredients:

- 1 lb shrimp, peeled and deveined
- 3 cups cooked rice (preferably cold)
- 2 tbsp soy sauce
- 2 tbsp sesame oil
- 1/2 cup peas and carrots (frozen or fresh)
- 2 eggs, scrambled
- 2 cloves garlic, minced
- 1 small onion, chopped
- 2 green onions, chopped
- Salt and pepper to taste

Instructions:

1. Heat sesame oil in a pan over medium-high heat. Cook shrimp for 2-3 minutes per side until pink and cooked through. Remove and set aside.
2. In the same pan, add garlic, onion, and peas and carrots. Stir-fry for 3-4 minutes.
3. Add cooked rice, soy sauce, and scrambled eggs. Stir-fry until well combined.
4. Add shrimp back to the pan and toss with green onions. Serve hot.

Chicken Quesadillas

Ingredients:

- 2 boneless, skinless chicken breasts, cooked and shredded
- 4 flour tortillas
- 1 cup shredded cheddar cheese
- 1 cup shredded mozzarella cheese
- 1/2 cup diced bell peppers
- 1/2 cup diced onions
- 1 tbsp olive oil
- 1 tsp cumin
- 1 tsp chili powder
- Salt and pepper to taste
- Sour cream and salsa for serving

Instructions:

1. Heat olive oil in a skillet over medium heat. Sauté bell peppers and onions until softened, about 3-4 minutes.
2. Add shredded chicken, cumin, chili powder, salt, and pepper to the skillet. Cook for 2 minutes, then remove from heat.
3. Heat a separate skillet over medium heat. Place one tortilla in the skillet and sprinkle with cheese, then add the chicken mixture on top. Place another tortilla on top.
4. Cook for 2-3 minutes per side, until the tortillas are golden brown and the cheese has melted. Slice into wedges and serve with sour cream and salsa.

Lemon Garlic Roasted Chicken

Ingredients:

- 1 whole chicken (about 4 lbs)
- 2 lemons, quartered
- 4 cloves garlic, smashed
- 1/4 cup olive oil
- 2 tbsp fresh thyme or rosemary
- Salt and pepper to taste

Instructions:

1. Preheat oven to 400°F (200°C). Pat the chicken dry and season generously with salt and pepper, inside and out.
2. Stuff the cavity with lemon wedges, garlic, and herbs. Drizzle the outside of the chicken with olive oil.
3. Roast in the oven for 1 hour 20 minutes, or until the internal temperature reaches 165°F (75°C).
4. Let rest for 10 minutes before carving and serving.

Baked Ziti

Ingredients:

- 1 lb ziti pasta
- 2 cups marinara sauce
- 2 cups ricotta cheese
- 2 cups shredded mozzarella cheese
- 1/2 cup grated Parmesan cheese
- 1 tsp dried basil
- 1 tsp dried oregano
- Salt and pepper to taste

Instructions:

1. Preheat oven to 375°F (190°C). Cook ziti pasta according to package instructions. Drain and set aside.
2. In a large bowl, mix cooked pasta, marinara sauce, ricotta cheese, mozzarella, Parmesan, basil, oregano, salt, and pepper.
3. Transfer the mixture to a greased baking dish and top with more mozzarella cheese.
4. Bake for 25-30 minutes, until the cheese is melted and bubbly. Serve hot.

Fish and Chips

Ingredients:

- 4 white fish fillets (such as cod or haddock)
- 1 cup flour
- 1 tsp baking powder
- 1 tsp salt
- 1 cup cold beer or sparkling water
- 4 large potatoes, peeled and cut into fries
- Vegetable oil for frying
- Salt for seasoning

Instructions:

1. Preheat oil in a deep fryer or large pot to 350°F (175°C).
2. In a bowl, whisk together flour, baking powder, and salt. Slowly add beer or sparkling water to form a smooth batter.
3. Dip fish fillets into the batter, then carefully fry them in the hot oil for 4-5 minutes, until golden brown. Remove and drain on paper towels.
4. Fry the potato fries until golden and crispy, about 4-5 minutes. Season with salt.
5. Serve the fish with fries, lemon wedges, and tartar sauce.

Beef Burritos

Ingredients:

- 1 lb ground beef
- 1 packet taco seasoning
- 1 cup cooked rice
- 1 cup black beans, drained and rinsed
- 1 cup shredded cheddar cheese
- 4 large flour tortillas
- 1/2 cup sour cream
- Salsa for serving

Instructions:

1. In a skillet, cook ground beef over medium heat until browned. Drain excess fat and stir in taco seasoning with a little water as directed on the packet.
2. Lay tortillas flat and layer each with cooked rice, black beans, beef mixture, and shredded cheese.
3. Roll up the tortillas tightly, folding in the sides as you go.
4. Serve with sour cream and salsa.

Turkey Meatballs with Spaghetti

Ingredients:

- 1 lb ground turkey
- 1/2 cup breadcrumbs
- 1/4 cup Parmesan cheese
- 1 egg
- 2 tbsp chopped parsley
- 2 cups marinara sauce
- 1 lb spaghetti
- Salt and pepper to taste

Instructions:

1. Preheat oven to 375°F (190°C). In a bowl, mix turkey, breadcrumbs, Parmesan, egg, parsley, salt, and pepper.
2. Form the mixture into meatballs and place them on a baking sheet. Bake for 20-25 minutes, until browned and cooked through.
3. In a pot, heat marinara sauce and add meatballs to simmer for 10 minutes.
4. Cook spaghetti according to package instructions and toss with sauce and meatballs before serving.

Chicken Tenders with Honey Mustard

Ingredients:

- 1 lb chicken tenders
- 1 cup breadcrumbs
- 1/2 cup all-purpose flour
- 2 eggs, beaten
- Salt and pepper to taste
- 1/4 cup honey
- 1/4 cup Dijon mustard
- 1 tbsp mayonnaise

Instructions:

1. Preheat oven to 400°F (200°C). Season chicken tenders with salt and pepper.
2. Dredge the chicken in flour, dip in beaten eggs, and coat in breadcrumbs. Arrange on a baking sheet.
3. Bake for 15-20 minutes, until golden and cooked through.
4. In a small bowl, mix honey, Dijon mustard, and mayonnaise to make the dipping sauce. Serve with chicken tenders.

Broccoli and Cheddar Stuffed Chicken

Ingredients:

- 4 boneless, skinless chicken breasts
- 1 cup cooked broccoli, chopped
- 1 cup shredded cheddar cheese
- 1/2 cup cream cheese
- 1 tbsp olive oil
- Salt and pepper to taste

Instructions:

1. Preheat oven to 375°F (190°C). Cut a pocket into each chicken breast.
2. In a bowl, mix chopped broccoli, cream cheese, and cheddar cheese.
3. Stuff the mixture into each chicken breast and secure with toothpicks.
4. Heat olive oil in a skillet over medium-high heat. Brown chicken on both sides, then transfer to the oven and bake for 20-25 minutes until cooked through.

Beef Stroganoff

Ingredients:

- 1 lb beef (sirloin or tenderloin), sliced into thin strips
- 1 onion, chopped
- 2 cloves garlic, minced
- 1 cup beef broth
- 1 cup sour cream
- 1 tbsp Worcestershire sauce
- 2 tbsp butter
- 1 tbsp flour
- Salt and pepper to taste
- 8 oz egg noodles

Instructions:

1. Cook egg noodles according to package instructions and set aside.
2. In a skillet, melt butter and sauté onions and garlic until soft. Add beef and cook until browned.
3. Sprinkle flour over beef and cook for 1 minute. Add beef broth, Worcestershire sauce, salt, and pepper, and simmer for 5-7 minutes.
4. Stir in sour cream and cook for another 2 minutes. Serve over the egg noodles.

Grilled Steak with Roasted Potatoes

Ingredients:

- 2 ribeye or sirloin steaks
- 4 medium potatoes, cubed
- 2 tbsp olive oil
- 1 tsp garlic powder
- 1 tsp dried rosemary
- Salt and pepper to taste
- 1 tbsp butter (optional)

Instructions:

1. Preheat grill to medium-high heat. Season steaks with salt, pepper, and rosemary.
2. Toss cubed potatoes with olive oil, garlic powder, salt, and pepper. Spread them on a baking sheet.
3. Roast potatoes at 400°F (200°C) for 20-25 minutes, flipping halfway through.
4. Grill steaks for 4-5 minutes per side, depending on desired doneness. Let rest for 5 minutes.
5. Serve steaks with roasted potatoes and a dollop of butter if desired.

Chicken and Vegetable Soup

Ingredients:

- 2 boneless, skinless chicken breasts, diced
- 4 cups chicken broth
- 2 carrots, sliced
- 2 celery stalks, diced
- 1 onion, chopped
- 1 tsp thyme
- Salt and pepper to taste
- 1 cup spinach or kale
- 1/2 cup small pasta (optional)

Instructions:

1. In a large pot, bring chicken broth to a boil. Add carrots, celery, and onion. Simmer for 10 minutes.
2. Add chicken, thyme, salt, and pepper. Cook until chicken is fully cooked, about 10 minutes.
3. Stir in spinach (or kale) and pasta (if using) and cook for another 5-7 minutes.
4. Serve hot, adjusting seasoning to taste.

Baked Chicken Wings

Ingredients:

- 10 chicken wings
- 2 tbsp olive oil
- 1 tsp garlic powder
- 1 tsp paprika
- 1/2 tsp cayenne pepper (optional)
- Salt and pepper to taste
- 1/4 cup BBQ sauce (optional)

Instructions:

1. Preheat oven to 400°F (200°C). Line a baking sheet with parchment paper.
2. Toss chicken wings with olive oil, garlic powder, paprika, cayenne, salt, and pepper.
3. Arrange wings on the baking sheet in a single layer. Bake for 25-30 minutes, turning halfway through.
4. Optional: Brush wings with BBQ sauce during the last 5 minutes of baking. Serve hot.

Beef and Cheese Tacos

Ingredients:

- 1 lb ground beef
- 1 packet taco seasoning
- 1/4 cup water
- 8 small flour tortillas
- 1 cup shredded cheddar cheese
- 1/2 cup lettuce, shredded
- 1/2 cup diced tomatoes
- 1/4 cup sour cream (optional)

Instructions:

1. In a skillet, cook ground beef over medium heat until browned. Drain excess fat.
2. Add taco seasoning and water to the beef. Simmer for 5 minutes.
3. Warm tortillas in a dry skillet or microwave.
4. Spoon beef mixture into tortillas and top with cheese, lettuce, tomatoes, and sour cream.
5. Serve immediately.

Spaghetti Carbonara

Ingredients:

- 1 lb spaghetti
- 4 oz pancetta or bacon, chopped
- 2 eggs
- 1 cup grated Parmesan cheese
- 2 cloves garlic, minced
- Salt and pepper to taste
- 1 tbsp olive oil

Instructions:

1. Cook spaghetti according to package directions. Drain, reserving 1 cup of pasta water.
2. In a skillet, heat olive oil over medium heat. Add pancetta and cook until crispy, about 5 minutes.
3. Add garlic to the pancetta and cook for 1 minute.
4. In a bowl, whisk eggs and Parmesan together. Add a bit of reserved pasta water to the egg mixture to temper it.
5. Toss hot pasta with pancetta and egg mixture. Add more pasta water if needed to create a creamy sauce.
6. Serve with extra Parmesan and pepper.

Baked Salmon with Lemon and Dill

Ingredients:

- 4 salmon fillets
- 1 lemon, sliced
- 2 tbsp fresh dill, chopped
- 2 tbsp olive oil
- Salt and pepper to taste

Instructions:

1. Preheat oven to 400°F (200°C). Place salmon fillets on a baking sheet lined with parchment paper.
2. Drizzle with olive oil, and sprinkle with salt, pepper, and chopped dill.
3. Top with lemon slices and bake for 12-15 minutes, or until the salmon flakes easily with a fork.
4. Serve with extra lemon wedges and garnish with fresh dill.

Pork Tenderloin with Roasted Brussels Sprouts

Ingredients:

- 1 pork tenderloin (about 1 lb)
- 2 cups Brussels sprouts, halved
- 2 tbsp olive oil
- 1 tsp garlic powder
- 1 tsp thyme
- Salt and pepper to taste

Instructions:

1. Preheat oven to 400°F (200°C). Season pork tenderloin with garlic powder, thyme, salt, and pepper.
2. Toss Brussels sprouts with olive oil, salt, and pepper. Spread them on a baking sheet.
3. Place the pork tenderloin on the same sheet or another baking dish.
4. Roast for 25-30 minutes, until the pork reaches an internal temperature of 145°F (63°C) and the Brussels sprouts are crispy.
5. Let the pork rest for 5 minutes before slicing. Serve with Brussels sprouts.

Vegetarian Stir-fry

Ingredients:

- 1 cup broccoli florets
- 1 bell pepper, sliced
- 1 carrot, julienned
- 1/2 cup snap peas
- 2 tbsp soy sauce
- 1 tbsp sesame oil
- 1 tbsp rice vinegar
- 1 tbsp hoisin sauce (optional)
- 1 tbsp sesame seeds (optional)
- Cooked rice for serving

Instructions:

1. Heat sesame oil in a large pan or wok over medium-high heat. Add broccoli, bell pepper, carrot, and snap peas.
2. Stir-fry for 5-7 minutes, until vegetables are tender-crisp.
3. Add soy sauce, rice vinegar, and hoisin sauce, if using. Stir to coat.
4. Serve over cooked rice and sprinkle with sesame seeds if desired.